W9-BRT-015

Snap books™

BABYSITTING

Babysitting SAFETY

PREVENTING ACCIDENTS AND INJURIES

by Barbara Mehlman

Consultant: Beth Lapp
Certified Babysitting Training Instructor

Capstone press®

Mankato, Minnesota

Snap Books are published by Capstone Press,
151 Good Counsel Drive, P.O. Box 669, Mankato, Minnesota 56002.
www.capstonepress.com

Library of Congress Cataloging-in-Publication Data

Mehlman, Barbara.

Babysitting safety: preventing accidents and injuries / Barbara Mehlman.

p. cm.—(Snap books. Babysitting)

Summary: "A guide for pre-teens and teens on safety and prevention of accidents while babysitting"—Provided by publisher.

Includes bibliographical references and index.

ISBN-13: 978-0-7368-6465-7 (hardcover)

ISBN-10: 0-7368-6465-2 (hardcover)

1. Babysitting—Juvenile literature. 2. Safety education—Juvenile education 3. Children's accidents—Prevention—Juvenile literature. I. Title II. Series

HQ769.5.M44 2007

649'.10248—dc22   2006001737

Editor: Becky Viaene

Designer: Jennifer Bergstrom

Photo Researcher/Photo Editor: Kelly Garvin

Photo Credits:

Barbara Mehlman, 32; Capstone Press/Karon Dubke, 7, 10–11, 13, 14–15, 18–19, 20–21, 27; Capstone Press/ TJ Thoraldson Digital Photography, cover; Corbis/Ariel Skelley, 17; Corbis/Joe Bator, 8–9; Getty Images Inc./ The Image Bank/Elyse Lewin, 4–5; Getty Images Inc./Taxi/Paul Conrath, 22–23; Index Stock Imagery/Novastock, 25; Photodisc, 16 (rubber duck); PhotoEdit Inc./David Young-Wolff, 28

1 2 3 4 5 6 11 10 09 08 07 06

Table of Contents

Staying Safe

You will hopefully never have to handle an emergency while you're babysitting. But no matter how careful you are, accidents and injuries can still happen.

This book will teach you about things that can go wrong while you're babysitting. It may sound scary, but don't be afraid. Along with learning how to handle safety issues, you'll also learn how to prevent them.

Parents trust you to take good care of their children. Do you know what it takes to be a safe sitter?

Making the House Safe

Look around the room. That pen cap and electric outlet don't look like toys to you. But to curious babies, many dangerous items look like tons of fun.

Almost all parents baby-proof their homes. They put gates across unsafe rooms, locks on cabinets, and plastic covers over electrical outlets. But somehow, little ones still get into dangerous situations.

What Can Go Wrong

Babies and toddlers put everything in their mouths. Exploring the world is exciting to them. If cabinets aren't locked, a small child could find poisonous products or pinch her fingers.

Helpful Hint

Before older kids put small blocks and puzzles away, count the pieces. Check the floor for missing pieces so small children don't find and swallow them.

Prevention

You can make a house safer by picking up things you see on the floor. A bead, a button, or a paper clip could mean danger. Check the child's toys for small, loose pieces. Even cuddly stuffed animals can be dangerous. Carefully check stuffed animals for loose eyes or buttons. Also, look for holes in squeaky toys. A child could choke on a tiny squeaker that falls out of a toy.

Some of the most poisonous items, like cleaning supplies, are hidden in drawers and cabinets. Make sure all cabinet doors are closed and locked. Have the number for the poison control center near the phone, in case you need to call for help.

You can also keep small children safe by closing doors or using gates to block unsafe rooms. Young children can really get hurt while exploring, but you can make sure they don't.

Helpful Hint

If a child comes in contact with poison, stay calm. Call the poison control center. Be prepared to answer questions about:

* The child's age and weight
* Poison name and amount that was swallowed
* Any health problems

Kitchen Chaos

Stoves, silverware, and glass dishes—the kitchen is one of the most dangerous places in the house.

What Can Go Wrong

Keep kids away from the stove. If you're cooking, the stove will be hot and a child could get burned. Toddlers can reach up and grab a pot handle as fast as you can blink.

Silverware is another danger. You know that children can hurt themselves with knives. But did you know that forks and spoons can be dangerous too?

TREATING BURNS

First aid for minor burns is simple. Run cold water over the burn for about two minutes. Gently pat the area dry and cover it with a loose bandage. If the burn is blistering, or the skin is discoloring, call the child's parents.

Glass dishes can be slippery and easy to drop. It can be hard to find the tiny pieces of broken glass. Sharp glass pieces that aren't found could end up cutting into little feet.

Prevention

When using the stove, put things on the back burners where little fingers can't reach the heat. If you must use a front burner, turn pot handles away from the edge. Then young kids can't grab pot handles and spill hot food on themselves.

Plastic is the solution to dangerous dishes and silverware. Even young children can safely use plastic silverware. If you give children plastic plates and cups, you'll never have to clean up broken glass.

CHAPTER 4

More Trouble in the Kitchen

In only a few minutes a child can choke or have an allergic reaction. Make sure you know what to do.

What Can Go Wrong

A child probably won't have an allergic reaction to food while you're babysitting. But just in case, look for these signs: trouble breathing after eating, breaking out in hives, dizziness, and swelling of the lips.

Prevention

Avoiding allergic reactions to food is easy. Parents usually will tell you if their child is allergic to certain foods. If they don't mention any food allergies, ask. If you know a child has a food allergy, check food labels before letting him eat anything.

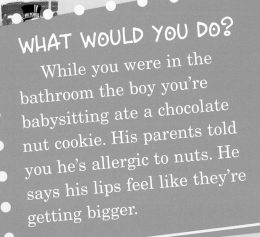

WHAT WOULD YOU DO?

While you were in the bathroom the boy you're babysitting ate a chocolate nut cookie. His parents told you he's allergic to nuts. He says his lips feel like they're getting bigger.

SIMPLE SOLUTION

Call the child's parents. You may need to give him a drug called antihistamine. Or he may need to drink lots of water to wash down the nuts. If the child is having trouble breathing, call 911 immediately.

What Else Can Go Wrong?

Young children love dangerous foods, like sticky candy and hotdogs. If they put too much food in their mouths, they can choke. Choking is a dangerous situation.

If the child is coughing while choking, let her keep coughing until she coughs up the piece of food. But if she's not making any sounds or isn't breathing, perform the Heimlich maneuver.

Prevention

One of the easiest ways to prevent choking is to avoid feeding children certain foods. Some foods to avoid are nuts, hard or sticky candy, grapes, popcorn, and hotdogs. But these aren't the only dangerous foods.

Anytime children put too much food in their mouths, it can be dangerous. Cut food into tiny pieces and make sure children take only one piece at a time. Make sure children sit down while eating and don't talk with food in their mouths.

PERFORMING THE HEIMLICH MANEUVER

1. Squat behind the child as she stands in front of you or put her on your lap.
2. Make a fist and place it in the middle of her belly. Place the thumb side of your fist just above the child's belly button.
3. Place your other hand on top of your first.
4. Pull upward forcefully, toward the child's nose, in a series of five quick thrusts.
5. Continue repeating the series of five thrusts until the child can breathe or the object is coughed up.

Beware of the Bathroom

Giving baths while babysitting can be fun, but it can be dangerous too. Most of the time you will not have to bathe children. But if they get dirty playing outside, they may need a bath.

What Can Go Wrong

Did you know that it's possible for a baby or toddler to drown in 1 inch (2.5 centimeters) of water? It seems unbelievable, but it's true. Bathtubs are slippery. If you're not watching closely, a baby could slip and become unconscious face-down in the water.

Another bathtub danger is water temperature. If the water temperature is too hot, the child's skin may get burned.

Prevention

The largest bathroom problem, drowning, is easy to prevent. The solution is to never leave a young child alone in a bathtub.

When you fill the tub, 4 to 5 inches (10 to 13 centimeters) of water is enough. Then dip your elbow in the water to test the temperature.

If you're bathing babies or toddlers, get a good grip when picking them up. Help children who are older than 4 years old out of the tub by holding their hands.

Helpful Hint

If giving a bath makes you nervous, just wash the child with a washcloth.

17

6 Fire

Fires can start and spread quickly. Make sure you know what to do in case of a fire.

What Can Go Wrong

Stoves, space heaters, and candles can all cause a house to burst into flames in only a few minutes. Anything that gets too close to the hot stove, including shirt sleeves, can catch on fire. Any room with a space heater or burning candle can be dangerous too. Curtains that are close to heaters or candles could quickly mean trouble.

Be Prepared

Discuss fire safety with a child's parents. Have them point out the smoke detectors. Ask if they have rope ladders for upstairs windows.

Some families even have a fire escape plan posted. Look at the fire escape plan or ask for a house tour so you know where the exits are. Being prepared will help you stay calm in case of an emergency.

FIRE
extinguisher

Prevention

You don't have to be a firefighter to prevent fires. Staying safe can be as simple as not using certain items. Blow out that candle. Avoid using the stove. Try heating food in the microwave instead. Make sure lighters and matches are kept out of the children's reach.

In the Event of a Fire

Since you aren't a firefighter, never try to put out a fire yourself. Your job is to get the children and yourself away from the fire as quickly as possible.

If you are trying to get out of a burning room, stay low to the ground so you don't breathe in smoke. Although it may be tough, try to stay calm. Call the fire department from a neighbor's house, and then call the children's parents.

WHAT WOULD YOU DO?

The boy you're babysitting is sleeping when the fire alarm goes off. You wake him and both get outside to a safe area. Soon he starts to cry. He wants you to go back inside the burning house and rescue his favorite toy.

SIMPLE SOLUTION

Don't go back inside for anything. Leave all toys, your purse, and anything else you think is valuable. Nothing is as valuable as you and the child.

Danger at the Door

Ding-dong. Someone is at the door. Although answering the door while you're babysitting may not seem like a big deal, you should be careful.

If the doorbell rings, don't answer it. If you hear strange noises outside, don't go out to check.

Safety is important when answering the phone too. If the phone rings, take a message. Don't give out information that the parents are gone. Say: "I'm sorry, but Mrs. Smith can't come to the phone just now. May I please take a message?" If you're not comfortable answering the phone, talk to the parents.

Helpful Hint

Leave an outside light and the TV or radio on. Then if someone comes to the door, they'll know the house isn't empty.

Safety Outside

It's a warm summer day, and the children can't wait to get outside. From biking to building sand castles, many fun activities can only be done outside.

What Can Go Wrong

Since children can do more active things outside, there's a greater chance of injuries and accidents. Scraped knees and elbows are common. Children could fall from a slide and break bones or become unconscious. They also may think it's OK to leave the yard without telling you.

Prevention

Serious accidents and injuries that require CPR are more likely to happen outside. A child who isn't breathing needs CPR. Prepare for emergencies by taking a CPR class before you begin babysitting.

You can reduce the number of outside accidents and injuries by watching children at all times. If a toddler wants to go on the slide, gently guide her down. Make sure to set boundaries so kids know to stay in the yard.

If you leave the yard, put young children in a stroller. Hold hands with older children when crossing the street. If you're cautious and prepared, playing outside can be safe and fun.

Bedtime Safety

The kids are in bed sleeping. But your job isn't over until the parents get back. You still need to check on the kids to make sure they're breathing OK and feeling safe.

What Can Go Wrong

Shortly after the children go to bed you quietly peek into their rooms. Usually you'll find the kids sleeping peacefully. But you might find them wide-awake, missing their parents or afraid of the dark. And with babies, there's always the danger of Sudden Infant Death Syndrome (SIDS). SIDS is the unexplained death of a baby who is younger than 1-year-old. SIDS usually affects 2 to 4 month old babies while they are sleeping.

Prevention

You can help prevent SIDS. Toys and pillows can cause babies to suffocate. Take these dangerous items out of cribs. Put sleeping babies on their backs, instead of their tummies, so they can't suffocate.

Check on babies every half hour. Many families have intercoms in babies' rooms.

Be sure the intercom volume is turned up. Then you can always hear what's going on.

But babies aren't the only ones you need to check on. Comfort scared kids by plugging in a night-light or reading a short story. Even once kids are asleep, check on them often.

You'll Do Fine!

Thinking about all the safety issues may seem like a lot to remember. Most accidents and injuries won't happen while you're babysitting. But just in case, you are now prepared to stay calm, think clearly, and handle many safety issues.

Checklist:

Being Prepared for an Emergency

When an emergency happens, you need to be prepared. Check the list below to see if you're ready.

✓ Have your emergency phone number sheet handy at all times. Numbers on the list should include: the children's parents, fire, police, and poison control.

✓ Know where to find a first aid kit.

✓ Have instruction sheets for the Heimlich maneuver and CPR where you can get to them quickly.

✓ Make a list of any allergies or health problems the children have.

✓ Memorize where all the exits are in case of fire.

✓ Always know where the phone is. You don't want to be searching for it during an emergency.

Glossary

CPR (cardiopulmonary resuscitation) (kar-dee-oh-PUHL-muh-nair-ee ree-se-se-TAY-shuhn)—a method of restarting a heart that has stopped beating; it involves breathing into a patient's mouth and pressing on a patient's chest in a certain rhythm.

Heimlich maneuver (HIME-lik muh-NOO-ver)—a safety procedure used to help someone who is choking

SIDS (Sudden Infant Death Syndrome) (SUHD-uhn In-funhnt DETH SIN-drohm)—sudden and unexpected death of an apparently healthy infant during sleep

suffocate (SUHF-uh-kate)—to die from lack of oxygen

Quick Tips

* Take a babysitting training course.

* Practice CPR and the Heimlich maneuver on a doll.

* Take a basic or youth first aid class.

* Never bring electrical appliances into the bathroom.

* Don't hesitate to call the parents if you need some help dealing with an accident or emergency.

* If a child spills on the floor, make sure that after wiping the floor you also dry it, so that no one slips.

* Keep a small flashlight in your purse or backpack so you'll be ready if the power goes out.

Read More

American Red Cross. *American Red Cross Babysitter's Handbook.* St. Louis: Mosby, 1998.

Dayee, Frances S. *Babysitting.* New York: Franklin Watts, 2000.

National Safety Council. *BLAST: Babysitter Lessons and Safety Training.* Sudbury, Mass.: Jones and Bartlett, 2003.

Raatma, Lucia. *Safety for Babysitters.* Living Well. Chanhassen, Minn.: Child's World, 2005.

Internet Sites

FactHound offers a safe, fun way to find Internet sites related to this book. All of the sites on FactHound have been researched by our staff.

Here's how:

1. Visit *www.facthound.com*

2. Choose your grade level.

3. Type in this book ID **0736864652** for age-appropriate sites. You may also browse subjects by clicking on letters, or by clicking on pictures and words.

4. Click on the **Fetch It** button.

Facthound will fetch the best sites for you!

About the Author

Barbara K. Mehlman began babysitting at 10 years old when her new baby brother was born. She continued to babysit all through high school and college to earn extra money, until she married and had two lovely daughters of her own.

Now she's a high school librarian and a newspaper columnist of a weekly theater column. In her spare time, she uses all the babysitting skills she writes about when she takes care of her four young grandchildren, whom she adores.

Index